ULTIMATE SOUP LOVER'S GUIDE

Delicious and Nutritious Recipes to Warm Your Soul

EMILY J. SMITH

COPYRIGHT 2024 © EMILY J. SMITH

All rights reserved. No part of this book may be reproduced, stored in retrieval system, or transmitted in any form or by any means, electronic, mechanical, photocopying, recording, or otherwise, without the prior written permission of the copyright holder, except in the case of brief quotations used in critical reviews or articles

TABLE OF CONTENTS

Introduction to Healthy Soups 5
   Benefits of Soup in a Healthy Diet 5
   Essential Tools and Ingredients 6
   Tips for Making Nutritious Soups 8
   Stock and Broth Basics 9
   Meal Planning and Preparation Tips 11

Chapter 1 13
   Classic Vegetable Soups 13
      Hearty Vegetable Soup 13
      Minestrone Soup 14
      Creamy Tomato Basil Soup 15
      Spinach and Kale Soup 17
      Root Vegetable Stew 18
      Mediterranean Lentil Soup 20

Chapter 2 22
   Protein Packed Soups 22
      Chicken and Quinoa Soup 22
      Beef and Barley Soup 23
      Turkey and White Bean Chili 25
      Lentil and Sausage Stew 26
      Tofu and Vegetable Soup 27
      Seafood Chowder 29

Chapter 3 31
   Low-calorie Soups 31
      Broccoli and Cauliflower Soup 31
      Cabbage Detox Soup 32
      Spicy Carrot and Ginger Soup 34
      Lemon Chicken Orzo Soup 35
      Tomato and Zucchini Soup 37
      Clear Vegetable Broth 38

Chapter 4 40
   Comforting Creamy Soups 40

- Creamy Mushroom Soup 40
- Sweet Potato and Coconut Soup 41
- Creamy Asparagus Soup 43
- Butternut Squash Soup 44
- Corn and Red Pepper Chowder 46
- Healthy Clam Chowder 47

Chapter 5 49

Immune Boosting Soups 49

- Garlic and Chicken Soup 49
- Spiced Turmeric Lentil Soup 50
- Ginger and Carrot Soup 52
- Immune Boosting Vegetable Soup 53
- Lemon and Herb Broth 54
- Green Detox Soup 56

Chapter 6 58

International Flavors 58

- Thai Coconut Chicken Soup 58
- Mexican Tortilla Soup 59
- Indian Spiced Lentil Soup 61
- Italian Minestrone Soup 62
- French Onion Soup 64
- Japanese Miso Soup 65

Chapter 7 67

Quick and Easy Soups 67

- 15Minute Tomato Basil Soup 67
- Instant Pot Vegetable Soup 68
- Quick Chickpea and Spinach Stew 69
- Fast Lentil and Carrot Soup 71
- Speedy Potato and Leek Soup 72
- Rapid Fire Gazpacho 74

Introduction to Healthy Soups

Benefits of Soup in a Healthy Diet

Soup can be a nutritious and beneficial addition to a healthy diet, offering several advantages:

1. Hydration: Soup helps meet daily fluid intake requirements, essential for maintaining proper bodily functions.

2. Weight Management: Low-calorie soups, especially vegetable-based ones, support weight loss and maintenance.

3. Nutrient-Dense: Soups can pack a high amount of essential vitamins, minerals, and antioxidants from vegetables, lean proteins, and whole grains.

4. Digestive Health: Broth-based soups, especially those with ginger and garlic, aid digestion and alleviate cold and flu symptoms.

5. Immune System Boost: Chicken soup, in particular, has been shown to have anti-inflammatory properties that help combat infections.

6. Anti-Inflammatory Effects: Certain soups, like tomato soup, contain antioxidants that reduce inflammation and may lower chronic disease risk.

7. Convenient Meal Option: Soup is an easy, portable meal choice, perfect for busy lifestyles.

8. Supports Healthy Gut Bacteria: Fermented soups, such as miso, promote beneficial gut bacteria.

9. Lowers Blood Pressure: Regular consumption of potassium-rich soups, like lentil or vegetable soup, can help reduce blood pressure.

10. Promotes Mindful Eating: Savoring a warm, comforting bowl of soup encourages slower eating and increased satisfaction.

To reap these benefits, focus on:

- Using lean proteins and vegetables
- Limiting cream, salt, and sugar
- Incorporating whole grains and legumes
- Choosing low-sodium broth
- Experimenting with various spices for added flavor

Essential Tools and Ingredients

Essential tools and ingredients can vary depending on the context, such as cooking, gardening, painting, or other activities. Here are some general essential tools and ingredients for a few common areas:

Cooking:

Tools:

1. Knives
2. Cutting boards
3. Pots and pans
4. Colander
5. Measuring cups and spoons
6. Can opener
7. Mixing bowls
8. Spatulas

Ingredients:

1. Salt
2. Pepper
3. Flour
4. Sugar
5. Olive oil
6. Garlic
7. Onions
8. Basic spices

Gardening:

Tools:

1. Gloves
2. Pruning shears
3. Watering can
4. Rake
5. Hoe
6. Trowel
7. Soil test kit

Ingredients:

1. Seeds
2. Fertilizer
3. Mulch
4. Compost
5. Soil conditioner

Painting:

Tools:

1. Brushes
2. Rollers
3. Paint trays
4. Palette
5. Easel
6. Rags
7. Paint thinner

Ingredients:

1. Paint
2. Primer
3. Varnish
4. Canvas or surface

First Aid Kit:

Tools:

1. Bandages
2. Gauze
3. Antiseptic wipes
4. Tweezers
5. Thermometer

Ingredients:

1. Antibiotic ointment
2. Pain relievers
3. Antihistamines
4. Band-Aid strips

Tips for Making Nutritious Soups

Servings: 4-6

Prep Time: 20 minutes

Cook Time: 30 minutes

Total Time: 50 minutes

Nutrition Information (per serving):

- Calories: 220
- Protein: 15g
- Fat: 8g
- Saturated Fat: 2.5g
- Cholesterol: 20mg
- Carbohydrates: 30g
- Fiber: 5g
- Sugar: 10g
- Sodium: 400mg

Ingredients:

- 2 tablespoons olive oil
- 1 onion, diced
- 3 cloves garlic, minced
- 3 carrots, peeled and sliced
- 2 celery stalks, sliced
- 2 cups mixed vegetables (zucchini, bell peppers, spinach)
- 4 cups low-sodium chicken broth
- 1 can (14.5 oz) diced tomatoes
- 1 teaspoon dried thyme
- 1/2 teaspoon dried basil
- Salt and pepper, to taste
- 1/2 cup low-fat cream (optional)

Directions:

1. Heat olive oil in a large pot over medium heat.
2. Add onion, garlic, carrots, and celery; cook until tender (8-10 minutes).
3. Add mixed vegetables, chicken broth, diced tomatoes, thyme, and basil.
4. Bring to a boil, then reduce heat and simmer (15-20 minutes).
5. Purée soup with an immersion blender or regular blender.

ents:

ock:

s (1-1.5 kg) bones (beef, chicken, fish, or pork)
ots, chopped
ery stalks, chopped
ves garlic, minced
gs fresh thyme
gs fresh parsley
 leaf
 black peppercorns
uarts (4-6 liters) water

oth:

s (1-1.5 kg) meat and bones (beef, chicken, fish, or pork)
rots, chopped
ery stalks, chopped
ves garlic, minced
igs fresh thyme
igs fresh parsley
 leaf
 black peppercorns
uarts (4-6 liters) water

ions:

heat oven to 400°F (200°C).
ast bones in the oven for 30 minutes to enhance flavor.
 large pot, combine roasted bones, chopped vegetables, herbs, and spices.
ur in water, covering all ingredients.
ng to a boil, then reduce heat to a simmer.
m impurities from surface.
mmer for 4-6 hours.
ain and discard solids.

mbine meat and bones, chopped vegetables, herbs, and spices in a large pot.
ur in water, covering all ingredients.
ng to a boil, then reduce heat to a simmer.

6. If desired, stir in low-fat cream for added creaminess.
7. Season with salt and pepper to taste.
8. Serve hot.

Tips for Making Nutritious Soups:

1. Choose low-sodium broth and limit added salt.
2. Incorporate a variety of colorful vegetables.
3. Use herbs and spices for flavor instead of excess salt or sugar.
4. Opt for lean protein sources (chicken, beans, lentils).
5. Experiment with plant-based cream alternatives (coconut milk, almond milk)
6. Consider roasting vegetables before adding to soup for enhanced flavor.
7. Make large batches and freeze for future meals.

Variations:

- Add protein: cooked chicken, beans, or tofu
- Spice it up: red pepper flakes or diced jalapeños
- Go green: add spinach, kale, or collard greens

Stock and Broth Basics

Stock and broth are fundamental components of many cuisines, serving as the sauces, and more. Learning to make stock and broth from scratch can elevate provide a rich, depthful flavor to your dishes.

Serving Size: 4-6 cups (1-1.5 liters)

Prep Time: 20 minutes

Cook Time: 4-6 hours (stock), 1-2 hours (broth)

Nutrition Information (per 1 cup serving):

- Calories: 10-20
- Protein: 1-2g
- Fat: 0-1g
- Sodium: 200-400mg
- Carbohydrates: 2-4g

4. Skim impurities from surface.
5. Simmer for 1-2 hours.
6. Strain and discard solids.

Tips and Variations:

- Use a mix of bones for a richer stock.
- Add acidity (vinegar, lemon juice) to extract minerals from bones.
- Experiment with different herbs and spices for unique flavor profiles.
- Store stock and broth in airtight containers in the fridge (3-5 days) or freezer (3-6 months).

Meal Planning and Preparation Tips

Meal Planning:

1. Set a budget and plan meals around sales.
2. Consider dietary restrictions and preferences.
3. Plan for leftovers to reduce waste.
4. Choose simple, versatile recipes.
5. Create a weekly or bi-weekly meal calendar.
6. Make a grocery list and stick to it.
7. Involve family members in meal planning.

Meal Preparation:

1. Prep ingredients in advance (chop, slice, dice).
2. Cook proteins and grains ahead of time.
3. Use a slow cooker or Instant Pot for convenience.
4. Roast vegetables for easy reheating.
5. Portion control for healthy eating.
6. Label and date leftovers.
7. Clean as you go to reduce cleanup time.

Time-Saving Tips:

1. Meal prep on weekends or one day a week.
2. Use one-pot wonders or sheet pan meals.
3. Keep a well-stocked pantry.
4. Freeze meals for future use.
5. Use a meal planning app or website.

Healthy Eating Tips:

1. Incorporate a variety of colorful vegetables.
2. Choose whole grains and lean proteins.
3. Limit processed and sugary foods.
4. Stay hydrated with water and herbal teas.
5. Cook with herbs and spices for added flavor.

Additional Resources:

- Meal planning apps: Plan to Eat, Yummly, or Mealime.
- Recipe websites: Allrecipes, Epicurious, or Food.com.
- Cookbooks or food blogs for inspiration.

Chapter 1

Classic Vegetable Soups

Hearty Vegetable Soup

Servings: 6-8

Prep Time: 20 minutes

Cook Time: 40 minutes

Total Time: 1 hour

Nutrition Information (per serving):

- Calories: 220
- Protein: 5g
- Fat: 9g
- Saturated Fat: 1g
- Cholesterol: 0mg
- Carbohydrates: 35g
- Fiber: 5g
- Sugar: 6g
- Sodium: 400mg

Ingredients:

- 2 tablespoons olive oil
- 1 onion, chopped (2 cups)
- 3 cloves garlic, minced (1 tablespoon)
- 3 carrots, chopped (2 cups)
- 2 potatoes, peeled and chopped (2 cups)
- 2 cups mixed vegetables (zucchini, bell peppers, green beans)
- 4 cups vegetable broth
- 2 cups diced tomatoes
- 1 teaspoon dried thyme
- 1 teaspoon dried rosemary
- Salt and pepper, to taste
- Fresh parsley, chopped (optional)

Directions:

1. In a large pot, heat olive oil over medium heat.
2. Add onion and garlic; cook until softened, 5 minutes.
3. Add carrots and potatoes; cook for 5 minutes.
4. Add mixed vegetables, vegetable broth, diced tomatoes, thyme, and rosemary.
5. Bring to a boil, then reduce heat and simmer, covered, for 25 minutes or until vegetables are tender.
6. Season with salt and pepper to taste.
7. Serve hot, garnished with chopped parsley if desired.

Tips and Variations:

- Use any combination of vegetables you like or have on hand.
- Add protein sources like cooked chicken, beans, or tofu for added nutrition.
- For a creamier soup, puree some or all of the vegetables.
- Store leftovers in the refrigerator for up to 3 days or freeze for up to 2 months.

Minestrone Soup

Servings: 6-8

Prep Time: 20 minutes

Cook Time: 40 minutes

Total Time: 1 hour

Nutrition Information (per serving):

- Calories: 220
- Protein: 18g
- Fat: 9g
- Saturated Fat: 1.5g
- Cholesterol: 0mg
- Carbohydrates: 30g
- Fiber: 6g
- Sugar: 6g
- Sodium: 400mg

Ingredients:

- 1 tablespoon olive oil
- 1 onion, chopped
- 3 cloves garlic, minced
- 2 medium carrots, chopped
- 2 celery stalks, chopped
- 1 (14.5 oz) can diced tomatoes
- 4 cups vegetable broth
- 1 can kidney beans, drained and rinsed
- 1 can cannellini beans, drained and rinsed
- 1 cup small pasta shapes (e.g., elbow macaroni)
- 1 teaspoon dried basil
- 1 teaspoon dried oregano
- Salt and pepper, to taste
- Grated Parmesan cheese, optional

Directions:

1. Heat olive oil in a large pot over medium heat.
2. Add onion, garlic, carrots, and celery; cook until vegetables are tender (8-10 minutes).
3. Add diced tomatoes, vegetable broth, kidney beans, cannellini beans, pasta, basil, oregano, salt, and pepper.
4. Bring to a boil, then reduce heat and simmer for 20-25 minutes or until pasta is al dente.
5. Taste and adjust seasoning.
6. Serve hot, topped with grated Parmesan cheese if desired.

Tips and Variations:

- Customize with your favorite vegetables or beans.
- Add cooked ground beef or sausage for added protein.
- Use low-sodium broth and tomatoes for reduced sodium content.
- Serve with crusty bread or a side salad.

Creamy Tomato Basil Soup

Servings: 4-6

Cooking Time: 25-30 minutes

Prep Time: 15 minutes

- 1/2 cup coconut milk or heavy cream (optional)
- 2 tablespoons freshly squeezed lemon juice
- Fresh herbs or scallions for garnish (optional)

Directions:

1. In a large pot, heat the olive oil over medium heat.
2. Add the chopped onion and cook until softened, about 5 minutes.
3. Add the minced garlic and cook for 1 minute.
4. Add the chopped kale and cook until wilted, about 3-4 minutes.
5. Add the spinach, cumin, smoked paprika (if using), salt, and pepper. Stir to combine.
6. Pour in the vegetable broth and bring the mixture to a boil.
7. Reduce heat to low and simmer for 15-20 minutes or until the greens are tender.
8. Use an immersion blender or transfer the soup to a blender and puree until smooth.
9. If desired, stir in coconut milk or heavy cream for added creaminess.
10. Stir in lemon juice and adjust seasoning.
11. Serve hot, garnished with fresh herbs or scallions (if desired).

Tips and Variations:

- For a creamier soup, add more coconut milk or heavy cream.
- Add diced chicken or beans for added protein.
- Substitute spinach with collard greens or other leafy greens.
- Serve with crusty bread or crackers for a satisfying meal.

Root Vegetable Stew

Serving Size: 6-8
Cooking Time: 45 minutes
Prep Time: 20 minutes

Nutrition Information (per serving):

- Calories: 240
- Fat: 8g
- Saturated Fat: 1g
- Cholesterol: 0mg
- Sodium: 400mg
- Carbohydrates: 38g
- Fiber: 6g
- Sugar: 8g

- 1 tablespoon olive oil
- 1 onion, chopped
- 3 cloves garlic, minced
- 2 medium carrots, chopped
- 2 celery stalks, chopped
- 1 (14.5 oz) can diced tomatoes
- 4 cups vegetable broth
- 1 can kidney beans, drained and rinsed
- 1 can cannellini beans, drained and rinsed
- 1 cup small pasta shapes (e.g., elbow macaroni)
- 1 teaspoon dried basil
- 1 teaspoon dried oregano
- Salt and pepper, to taste
- Grated Parmesan cheese, optional

Directions:

1. Heat olive oil in a large pot over medium heat.
2. Add onion, garlic, carrots, and celery; cook until vegetables are tender (8-10 minutes).
3. Add diced tomatoes, vegetable broth, kidney beans, cannellini beans, pasta, basil, oregano, salt, and pepper.
4. Bring to a boil, then reduce heat and simmer for 20-25 minutes or until pasta is al dente.
5. Taste and adjust seasoning.
6. Serve hot, topped with grated Parmesan cheese if desired.

Tips and Variations:

- Customize with your favorite vegetables or beans.
- Add cooked ground beef or sausage for added protein.
- Use low-sodium broth and tomatoes for reduced sodium content.
- Serve with crusty bread or a side salad.

Creamy Tomato Basil Soup

Servings: 4-6

Cooking Time: 25-30 minutes

Prep Time: 15 minutes

Nutrition Information (per serving):

- Calories: 220
- Total Fat: 10g
- Saturated Fat: 6g
- Cholesterol: 20mg
- Sodium: 450mg
- Total Carbohydrates: 25g
- Dietary Fiber: 4g
- Sugars: 12g
- Protein: 10g

Ingredients:

- 2 tablespoons butter
- 1 medium onion, chopped
- 3 cloves garlic, minced
- 2 cups chopped fresh tomatoes (or 1 can of diced tomatoes)
- 1 cup chicken or vegetable broth
- 1 cup heavy cream or half-and-half
- 1 tablespoon dried basil
- 1 teaspoon dried oregano
- Salt and pepper, to taste
- Fresh basil leaves, chopped (optional)

Directions:

1. In a large pot, melt butter over medium heat. Add onion and cook until softened (5 minutes).

2. Add garlic and cook for an additional minute.

3. Add chopped tomatoes, broth, basil, oregano, salt, and pepper. Bring to a boil, then reduce heat and simmer (15 minutes).

4. Use an immersion blender or transfer soup to a blender and puree until smooth.

5. Return soup to pot and stir in heavy cream or half-and-half. Heat over low heat until warmed through.

6. Taste and adjust seasoning.

7. Serve hot, garnished with chopped fresh basil leaves if desired.

Tips:

- For a lighter version, substitute heavy cream with Greek yogurt or coconut cream.
- Add grilled chicken or pasta for added protein and texture.
- Use fresh tomatoes during peak season for enhanced flavor.

Spinach and Kale Soup

Servings: 4-6
Prep Time: 20 minutes
Cook Time: 25 minutes
Total Time: 45 minutes

Nutrition Information (per serving):

- Calories: 170
- Protein: 15g
- Fat: 7g
- Saturated Fat: 1g
- Cholesterol: 0mg
- Carbohydrates: 20g
- Fiber: 4g
- Sugar: 2g
- Sodium: 400mg
- Vitamin A: 200% DV
- Vitamin C: 100% DV
- Calcium: 10% DV
- Iron: 20% DV

Ingredients:

- 2 cups chopped kale, stems removed and discarded, leaves coarsely chopped
- 2 cups fresh spinach leaves
- 2 tablespoons olive oil
- 1 onion, chopped
- 3 cloves garlic, minced
- 1 teaspoon ground cumin
- 1 teaspoon smoked paprika (optional)
- 1/2 teaspoon salt
- 1/4 teaspoon black pepper
- 4 cups vegetable broth

- 1/2 cup coconut milk or heavy cream (optional)
- 2 tablespoons freshly squeezed lemon juice
- Fresh herbs or scallions for garnish (optional)

Directions:

1. In a large pot, heat the olive oil over medium heat.
2. Add the chopped onion and cook until softened, about 5 minutes.
3. Add the minced garlic and cook for 1 minute.
4. Add the chopped kale and cook until wilted, about 3-4 minutes.
5. Add the spinach, cumin, smoked paprika (if using), salt, and pepper. Stir to combine.
6. Pour in the vegetable broth and bring the mixture to a boil.
7. Reduce heat to low and simmer for 15-20 minutes or until the greens are tender.
8. Use an immersion blender or transfer the soup to a blender and puree until smooth.
9. If desired, stir in coconut milk or heavy cream for added creaminess.
10. Stir in lemon juice and adjust seasoning.
11. Serve hot, garnished with fresh herbs or scallions (if desired).

Tips and Variations:

- For a creamier soup, add more coconut milk or heavy cream.
- Add diced chicken or beans for added protein.
- Substitute spinach with collard greens or other leafy greens.
- Serve with crusty bread or crackers for a satisfying meal.

Root Vegetable Stew

Serving Size: 6-8
Cooking Time: 45 minutes
Prep Time: 20 minutes

Nutrition Information (per serving):

- Calories: 240
- Fat: 8g
- Saturated Fat: 1g
- Cholesterol: 0mg
- Sodium: 400mg
- Carbohydrates: 38g
- Fiber: 6g
- Sugar: 8g

- Protein: 3g

Ingredients:

- 2 tablespoons olive oil
- 1 onion, chopped
- 3 cloves garlic, minced
- 2 carrots, peeled and chopped
- 2 parsnips, peeled and chopped
- 2 turnips, peeled and chopped
- 2 potatoes, peeled and chopped
- 1 large sweet potato, peeled and chopped
- 4 cups vegetable broth
- 1 teaspoon dried thyme
- 1 teaspoon dried rosemary
- Salt and pepper to taste
- 2 bay leaves (optional)

Directions:

1. Heat olive oil in a large Dutch oven over medium heat.

2. Add onion and garlic; cook until softened (5 minutes).

3. Add carrots, parsnips, turnips, potatoes, and sweet potato. Cook for 10 minutes.

4. Pour in vegetable broth and add thyme, rosemary, salt, pepper, and bay leaves (if using).

5. Bring to a boil, then reduce heat to low and simmer, covered, for 25-30 minutes or until vegetables are tender.

6. Remove bay leaves (if used) and serve hot.

Tips and Variations:

- For added protein, include cooked beans, lentils, or diced chicken.
- Spice up with red pepper flakes or sliced jalapeños.
- Use other root vegetables like beets or rutabaga.
- Serve with crusty bread or over mashed potatoes.

Mediterranean Lentil Soup

Servings: 6-8

Prep Time: 20 minutes

Cook Time: 40 minutes

Total Time: 1 hour

Nutrition Information (per serving):

- Calories: 250
- Protein: 18g
- Fat: 9g
- Saturated Fat: 1g
- Cholesterol: 0mg
- Carbohydrates: 35g
- Fiber: 10g
- Sugar: 6g
- Sodium: 400mg

Ingredients:

- 1 cup dried green or brown lentils, rinsed and drained
- 4 cups vegetable broth
- 2 cups water
- 2 tablespoons olive oil
- 1 onion, chopped
- 3 cloves garlic, minced
- 2 carrots, chopped
- 2 celery stalks, chopped
- 1 can (14.5 oz) diced tomatoes
- 1 teaspoon dried thyme
- 1 teaspoon dried oregano
- 1 bay leaf
- Salt and pepper, to taste
- 2 tablespoons fresh parsley, chopped (optional)
- 2 tablespoons lemon juice (optional)
- Feta cheese, crumbled (optional)

Directions:

1. In a large pot, heat the olive oil over medium heat.
2. Add the onion, garlic, carrots, and celery and cook until the vegetables are tender, about 8 minutes.
3. Add the lentils, vegetable broth, water, diced tomatoes, thyme, oregano, and bay leaf.
4. Bring to a boil, then reduce the heat to low and simmer, covered, for 30 minutes, or until the lentils are tender.
5. Season with salt and pepper to taste.
6. Serve hot, garnished with parsley, lemon juice, and feta cheese, if desired.

Tips and Variations:

- Use red or yellow lentils for a slightly different texture.
- Add other vegetables, such as zucchini or spinach, for added flavor and nutrition.
- Serve with a side of crusty bread or over rice or quinoa.
- Make ahead and refrigerate or freeze for up to 3 days.

Chapter 2

Protein Packed Soups

Chicken and Quinoa Soup

Servings: 4-6

Prep Time: 20 minutes

Cook Time: 35-40 minutes

Total Time: 55-60 minutes

Nutrition Information (per serving):

- Calories: 420
- Protein: 37g
- Fat: 20g
- Saturated Fat: 3.5g
- Cholesterol: 60mg
- Carbohydrates: 30g
- Fiber: 4g
- Sugar: 2g
- Sodium: 450mg

Ingredients:

- 1 pound boneless, skinless chicken breast or thighs
- 2 cups chicken broth
- 1 cup quinoa, rinsed and drained
- 1 large onion, diced
- 3 cloves garlic, minced
- 2 medium carrots, peeled and sliced
- 2 stalks celery, sliced
- 1 teaspoon dried thyme
- 1/2 teaspoon dried basil
- 1/2 teaspoon salt
- 1/4 teaspoon black pepper
- 2 tablespoons olive oil

Directions:

1. In a large pot or Dutch oven, heat the olive oil over medium heat.
2. Add the diced onion, minced garlic, sliced carrots, and sliced celery. Cook until the vegetables are tender, about 5-7 minutes.
3. Add the chicken to the pot and cook until browned on all sides, about 5-6 minutes.
4. Add the chicken broth, quinoa, thyme, basil, salt, and pepper to the pot.
5. Bring the mixture to a boil, then reduce the heat to low and simmer for 20-25 minutes, or until the quinoa is tender and the chicken is cooked through.
6. Remove the chicken from the pot and shred or chop it into bite-sized pieces. Return the chicken to the pot.
7. Serve hot, garnished with chopped fresh herbs, if desired.

Tips and Variations:

- Use low-sodium chicken broth to reduce the sodium content of the soup.
- Add diced bell peppers or mushrooms for extra flavor and nutrients.
- Substitute other whole grains, such as brown rice or farro, for the quinoa.
- Make the soup ahead and refrigerate or freeze for later use.

Quinoa Cooking Tips:

- Rinse quinoa before cooking to remove saponins, which can give it a bitter taste.
- Use a 2:1 ratio of liquid to quinoa.
- Cook quinoa until it's tender and the water has been absorbed.

Beef and Barley Soup

Servings: 6-8

Prep Time: 20 minutes

Cook Time: 1 hour 30 minutes

Total Time: 1 hour 50 minutes

Nutrition Information (per serving):

- Calories: 340
- Protein: 35g
- Fat: 12g
- Saturated Fat: 3.5g

- Cholesterol: 60mg
- Carbohydrates: 30g
- Fiber: 4g
- Sodium: 450mg

Ingredients:

- 2 pounds beef stew meat (cut into 1-inch pieces)
- 2 tablespoons olive oil
- 1 onion, chopped
- 3 cloves garlic, minced
- 2 carrots, peeled and chopped
- 2 celery stalks, chopped
- 1 cup pearl barley
- 4 cups beef broth
- 2 cups water
- 1 teaspoon dried thyme
- 1 teaspoon dried rosemary
- 1 bay leaf
- Salt and pepper, to taste

Directions:

1. Heat the olive oil in a large Dutch oven over medium-high heat.
2. Add the beef and cook until browned, about 5 minutes. Remove from pot and set aside.
3. Add the onion, garlic, carrots, and celery to the pot. Cook until the vegetables are tender, about 10 minutes.
4. Add the barley, beef broth, water, thyme, rosemary, and bay leaf to the pot. Stir to combine.
5. Return the beef to the pot and bring to a boil.
6. Reduce heat to low and simmer, covered, for 1 hour 15 minutes, or until the beef is tender.
7. Season with salt and pepper to taste.
8. Serve hot, garnished with fresh herbs if desired.

Tips and Variations:

- Use leaner beef cuts, such as sirloin or round, for a healthier option.
- Add diced potatoes or other root vegetables for added flavor and nutrition.
- Substitute mushrooms or other vegetables for the carrots and celery.
- For a quicker cook time, use instant barley or pressure cooker.

Turkey and White Bean Chili

Servings: 6-8

Prep Time: 20 minutes

Cook Time: 30-40 minutes

Total Time: 50-60 minutes

Nutrition Information (per serving):

- Calories: 350
- Protein: 37g
- Fat: 10g
- Saturated Fat: 2.5g
- Cholesterol: 60mg
- Carbohydrates: 30g
- Fiber: 6g
- Sodium: 400mg

Ingredients:

- 1 lb ground turkey breast
- 1 large onion, diced
- 3 cloves garlic, minced
- 1 red bell pepper, diced
- 2 cans (15 oz each) cannellini beans, drained and rinsed
- 1 can (14.5 oz) diced tomatoes
- 1 cup chicken broth
- 1 tsp ground cumin
- 1 tsp chili powder
- 1/2 tsp paprika
- Salt and pepper, to taste
- Optional: jalapenos, sour cream, shredded cheese, and diced avocado for toppings

Directions:

1. In a large pot or Dutch oven, heat 1 tablespoon of olive oil over medium-high heat.
2. Add the ground turkey and cook, breaking it up with a spoon, until browned, about 5-7 minutes.
3. Add the onion, garlic, and red bell pepper to the pot. Cook until the vegetables are tender, about 5 minutes.
4. Stir in cumin, chili powder, and paprika. Cook for 1 minute.

5. Add the cannellini beans, diced tomatoes, and chicken broth to the pot.
6. Bring the mixture to a simmer, then reduce the heat to low and cook for 20-25 minutes or until the flavors have melded together.
7. Season with salt and pepper to taste.
8. Serve hot, topped with desired toppings such as jalapenos, sour cream, shredded cheese, and diced avocado.

Tips and Variations:

- For a spicier chili, add diced jalapenos or serrano peppers.
- For a thicker chili, reduce the chicken broth or add a slurry of cornstarch and water.
- Experiment with different types of beans or add some diced potatoes for added texture.

Lentil and Sausage Stew

Servings: 6-8

Prep Time: 20 minutes

Cook Time: 40 minutes

Total Time: 1 hour

Nutrition Information (per serving):

- Calories: 540
- Protein: 37g
- Fat: 24g
- Saturated Fat: 8g
- Cholesterol: 60mg
- Carbohydrates: 40g
- Fiber: 10g
  Sugar: 2g
- Sodium: 450mg

Ingredients:

- 1 lb sweet Italian sausage, sliced
- 1 large onion, chopped
- 3 cloves garlic, minced
- 2 carrots, peeled and chopped
- 2 celery stalks, chopped

- 1 cup dried green or brown lentils, rinsed and drained
- 4 cups chicken broth
- 1 can (14.5 oz) diced tomatoes
- 1 tsp dried thyme
- 1 tsp dried rosemary
- 1 bay leaf
- Salt and pepper, to taste
- Olive oil, for cooking

Directions:

1. Heat olive oil in a large Dutch oven over medium-high heat.
2. Cook sausage until browned, about 5 minutes. Remove from pot and set aside.
3. Add onion, garlic, carrots, and celery to pot. Cook until vegetables are tender, about 5 minutes.
4. Add lentils, chicken broth, diced tomatoes, thyme, rosemary, and bay leaf to pot. Stir to combine.
5. Return sausage to pot and bring mixture to a boil.
6. Reduce heat to low and simmer, covered, for 30 minutes or until lentils are tender.
7. Season with salt and pepper to taste.
8. Serve hot, garnished with fresh herbs if desired.

Tips and Variations:

- Use red or yellow lentils for a slightly different texture.
- Add other vegetables like potatoes or zucchini for added flavor.
- Substitute chicken or vegetable broth for a lighter flavor.
- Serve with crusty bread or over rice or egg noodles.

Tofu and Vegetable Soup

Servings: 4-6

Prep Time: 15 minutes

Cook Time: 25 minutes

Total Time: 40 minutes

Nutrition Information (per serving):

- Calories: 220
- Protein: 20g
- Fat: 8g

- Saturated Fat: 1g
- Cholesterol: 0mg
- Carbohydrates: 25g
- Fiber: 4g
- Sugar: 6g
- Sodium: 400mg

Ingredients:

- 1 block of firm tofu, drained and cut into small cubes
- 2 tablespoons of vegetable oil
- 1 onion, chopped
- 3 cloves of garlic, minced
- 2 carrots, peeled and sliced
- 2 celery stalks, sliced
- 2 cups of mixed vegetables (such as bell peppers, zucchini, and mushrooms)
- 4 cups of vegetable broth
- 1 teaspoon of soy sauce
- 1 teaspoon of dried thyme
- Salt and pepper, to taste
- Fresh green onions, chopped (optional)

Directions:

1. Heat the oil in a large pot over medium heat.
2. Add the onion and garlic and cook until softened, about 3-4 minutes.
3. Add the carrots and celery and cook for an additional 4-5 minutes.
4. Add the mixed vegetables, vegetable broth, soy sauce, and thyme.
5. Bring the mixture to a boil, then reduce heat and simmer for 15 minutes.
6. Add the tofu and cook for an additional 5-7 minutes, or until heated through.
7. Season with salt and pepper to taste.
8. Serve hot, garnished with chopped green onions if desired.

Tips and Variations:

- Customize with your favorite vegetables or add noodles for added texture.
- For a spicy kick, add red pepper flakes or sliced jalapeños.
- Use low-sodium broth for a healthier option.
- Serve with crusty bread or crackers for a filling meal.

Storage and Reheating:

- Refrigerate for up to 3 days or freeze for up to 2 months.
- Reheat over low heat, adding additional broth if needed.

Seafood Chowder

Serving Size: 6-8

Prep Time: 20 minutes

Cook Time: 25 minutes

Total Time: 45 minutes

Nutrition Information (per serving):

- Calories: 340
- Protein: 30g
- Fat: 18g
- Saturated Fat: 10g
- Cholesterol: 60mg
- Sodium: 450mg
- Carbohydrates: 20g
- Fiber: 2g
- Sugar: 4g

Ingredients:

- 2 tablespoons butter
- 1 medium onion, diced
- 3 cloves garlic, minced
- 1 medium potato, peeled and diced
- 1 cup all-purpose flour
- 1 cup milk
- 1/2 cup heavy cream
- 1/2 cup fish stock
- 1 teaspoon dried thyme
- 1/2 teaspoon paprika
- 1/2 teaspoon salt
- 1/4 teaspoon black pepper
- 1 pound shrimp, peeled and deveined
- 1 pound scallops
- 1/2 pound cod, cut into bite-sized pieces

Directions:

1. Melt butter in a large pot over medium heat.

2. Add onion and garlic; cook until softened (5 minutes).
3. Add potato; cook for 2-3 minutes.
4. Stir in flour; cook for 1 minute.
5. Gradually add milk, heavy cream, and fish stock; whisk until smooth.
6. Bring mixture to a simmer; cook until thickened (5-7 minutes).
7. Add thyme, paprika, salt, and pepper.
8. Add shrimp, scallops, and cod; cook until seafood is cooked through (5-7 minutes).
9. Serve hot, garnished with chopped parsley or chives (optional).

Tips and Variations:

- Use fresh or frozen seafood.
- Substitute other seafood options like mussels or crab.
- Add diced bell peppers or carrots for extra flavor.
- For a creamier chowder, add more heavy cream.
- Serve with crusty bread or crackers.

Chapter 3

Low-calorie Soups

Broccoli and Cauliflower Soup

Servings: 4-6

Prep Time: 20 minutes

Cook Time: 25 minutes

Total Time: 45 minutes

Nutrition Information (per serving):

- Calories: 180
- Fat: 10g
- Saturated Fat: 2.5g
- Cholesterol: 20mg
- Sodium: 400mg
- Carbohydrates: 20g
- Fiber: 5g
- Protein: 5g
- Sugar: 5g

Ingredients:

- 2 tablespoons butter
- 1 onion, chopped
- 3 cloves garlic, minced
- 4 cups broccoli florets
- 2 cups cauliflower florets
- 2 cups chicken or vegetable broth
- 1 cup heavy cream or half-and-half (optional)
- 1 teaspoon dried thyme
- Salt and pepper, to taste
- Fresh parsley or chives, for garnish (optional)

Directions:

1. In a large pot, melt butter over medium heat. Add onion and cook until softened, about 5 minutes.

2. Add garlic and cook for 1 minute.

3. Add broccoli and cauliflower; cook, stirring occasionally, for 5 minutes.

4. Pour in broth and bring to a boil. Reduce heat and simmer until vegetables are tender, about 15 minutes.

5. Use an immersion blender or transfer soup to a blender and puree until smooth.

6. If desired, stir in heavy cream or half-and-half.

7. Season with thyme, salt, and pepper.

8. Serve hot, garnished with parsley or chives if desired.

Variations:

- For a creamier soup, add more heavy cream or half-and-half.
- For a lighter soup, use less cream or substitute with Greek yogurt.
- Add diced potatoes or carrots for added thickness and flavor.
- Use roasted broccoli and cauliflower for deeper flavor; simply toss with olive oil, salt, and pepper, and roast at 425°F (220°C) for 20 minutes.

Tips:

- Freeze soup for up to 3 months.
- Make ahead and refrigerate for up to 24 hours.
- Serve with crusty bread or crackers for a satisfying meal.

Cabbage Detox Soup

Servings: 4-6

Prep Time: 20 minutes

Cooking Time: 30 minutes

Total Time: 50 minutes

Nutrition Information (per serving):

- Calories: 120
- Protein: 5g
- Fat: 2g
- Saturated Fat: 0.5g
- Cholesterol: 0mg
- Carbohydrates: 25g
- Fiber: 5g
- Sugar: 6g
- Sodium: 400mg
- Potassium: 600mg
- Vitamin A: 20% of the Daily Value (DV)
- Vitamin C: 50% of the DV
- Vitamin K: 100% of the DV

Ingredients:

- 1 medium cabbage, chopped
- 2 medium carrots, chopped
- 2 stalks celery, chopped
- 1 medium onion, chopped
- 4 cloves garlic, minced
- 4 cups vegetable broth (low-sodium)
- 1 cup diced tomatoes
- 1 teaspoon dried thyme
- 1/2 teaspoon dried parsley
- 1/2 teaspoon salt
- 1/4 teaspoon black pepper
- 2 tablespoons olive oil (optional)

Directions:

1. In a large pot, heat the olive oil over medium heat.
2. Add the chopped onion, carrots, and celery, and cook until tender (5-7 minutes).
3. Add the minced garlic and cook for an additional minute.
4. Add the chopped cabbage, vegetable broth, diced tomatoes, thyme, parsley, salt, and pepper.
5. Bring the mixture to a boil, then reduce heat and simmer for 20-25 minutes or until the cabbage is tender.
6. Use an immersion blender to puree the soup until smooth, or let it cool and blend in a blender.
7. Serve hot, garnished with chopped fresh herbs (optional).

Tips and Variations:

- For added protein, add cooked chicken, beans, or tofu.
- Substitute spinach or kale for cabbage.
- Add a squeeze of fresh lemon juice for extra flavor.
- Store leftovers in the refrigerator for up to 3 days or freeze for up to 2 months.

Spicy Carrot and Ginger Soup

Servings: 4-6
Prep Time: 20 minutes
Cook Time: 30 minutes
Total Time: 50 minutes

Nutrition Information (per serving):

- Calories: 150
- Protein: 2g
- Fat: 7g
- Saturated Fat: 1g
- Cholesterol: 0mg
- Carbohydrates: 24g
- Fiber: 4g
- Sugar: 8g
- Sodium: 400mg

Ingredients:

- 2 tablespoons olive oil
- 1 medium onion, chopped
- 3 cloves garlic, minced
- 2 inches fresh ginger, peeled and grated
- 4 cups chopped carrots (about 6 medium)
- 2 teaspoons ground cumin
- 1 teaspoon smoked paprika
- 1/2 teaspoon ground cayenne pepper
- 1/2 teaspoon salt
- 1/4 teaspoon black pepper
- 4 cups vegetable broth
- 1/2 cup coconut milk (optional)
- Fresh cilantro or scallions for garnish

Directions:

1. In a large pot, heat the olive oil over medium heat.

2. Add the onion and cook until softened, about 5 minutes.

3. Add the garlic and ginger; cook for 1 minute.

4. Add the carrots, cumin, smoked paprika, cayenne pepper, salt, and black pepper. Cook for 5 minutes.

5. Pour in the vegetable broth and bring to a boil.

6. Reduce heat and simmer until the carrots are tender, about 20 minutes.

7. Purée the soup with an immersion blender or transfer to a blender.

8. If using coconut milk, stir it in after blending.

9. Taste and adjust seasoning.

10. Serve hot, garnished with cilantro or scallions.

Tips and Variations:

- For a creamier soup, add more coconut milk.
- Substitute carrots with sweet potatoes or parsnips.
- Adjust cayenne pepper to desired spice level.
- Serve with crusty bread or crackers.

Lemon Chicken Orzo Soup

Servings: 6-8

Prep Time: 20 minutes

Cook Time: 30 minutes

Total Time: 50 minutes

Nutrition Information (per serving):

- Calories: 320
- Protein: 36g
- Fat: 12g
- Saturated Fat: 2.5g
- Cholesterol: 60mg
- Carbohydrates: 25g
- Fiber: 2g
- Sugar: 2g
- Sodium: 450mg

Ingredients:

- 1 pound boneless, skinless chicken breast or thighs, cut into bite-sized pieces
- 4 cups chicken broth
- 2 cups water
- 1 cup orzo pasta
- 2 tablespoons olive oil
- 1 onion, diced
- 3 cloves garlic, minced
- 1 cup sliced carrots
- 1 cup sliced celery
- 1 teaspoon dried thyme
- 1/2 teaspoon dried basil
- 2 lemons, juiced (about 2 tablespoons)
- Salt and pepper, to taste
- Grated Parmesan cheese, for serving (optional)

Directions:

1. In a large pot or Dutch oven, heat the olive oil over medium heat.
2. Add the chicken and cook until browned, about 5-7 minutes. Remove from pot and set aside.
3. Add the diced onion, garlic, carrots, and celery to the pot. Cook until the vegetables are tender, about 5-7 minutes.
4. Add the chicken broth, water, orzo pasta, thyme, and basil to the pot. Stir to combine.
5. Return the chicken to the pot and bring to a boil.
6. Reduce heat to low and simmer for 15-20 minutes, or until the orzo is tender and the chicken is cooked through.
7. Stir in the lemon juice and season with salt and pepper to taste.
8. Serve hot, topped with grated Parmesan cheese if desired.

Tips and Variations:

- For an extra burst of citrus flavor, add slices of lemon to the pot during the last 5 minutes of cooking.

- Substitute chicken with turkey or vegetables for a vegetarian option.
- Add other vegetables, such as diced bell peppers or zucchini, for added flavor and nutrition.
- Serve with a side of crusty bread or crackers for dipping in the broth.

Tomato and Zucchini Soup

Servings: 4-6 people

Prep Time: 20 minutes

Cook Time: 30 minutes

Total Time: 50 minutes

Nutrition Information (per serving):

- Calories: 120
- Protein: 2g
- Fat: 7g
- Saturated Fat: 1g
- Cholesterol: 0mg
- Carbohydrates: 18g
- Fiber: 4g
- Sugar: 10g
- Sodium: 250mg

Ingredients:

- 2 medium zucchinis, chopped
- 2 medium tomatoes, chopped (or 1 can of diced tomatoes)
- 2 tablespoons olive oil
- 1 onion, chopped
- 3 cloves garlic, minced
- 4 cups vegetable broth
- 1 teaspoon dried basil
- 1 teaspoon dried oregano
- Salt and pepper, to taste
- 1/4 cup grated Parmesan cheese (optional)

Directions:

1. In a large pot, heat olive oil over medium heat.

2. Add chopped onion and sauté until softened, about 5 minutes.
3. Add minced garlic and cook for 1 minute.
4. Add chopped zucchinis and cook until tender, about 5 minutes.
5. Add chopped tomatoes, vegetable broth, basil, oregano, salt, and pepper.
6. Bring mixture to a boil, then reduce heat and simmer for 15-20 minutes.
7. Use an immersion blender or transfer soup to a blender and puree until smooth.
8. Taste and adjust seasoning as needed.
9. Serve hot, topped with grated Parmesan cheese if desired.

Tips and Variations:

- For a creamier soup, add 1/4 cup heavy cream or Greek yogurt.
- Add other vegetables like bell peppers or spinach for added flavor.
- Use fresh herbs instead of dried for enhanced flavor.
- Serve with crusty bread or crackers for a satisfying meal.

Clear Vegetable Broth

Servings: 4-6

Prep Time: 15 minutes

Cook Time: 30-40 minutes

Total Time: 45-55 minutes

Nutrition Information (per serving):

- Calories: 45
- Protein: 2g
- Fat: 0g
- Saturated Fat: 0g
- Cholesterol: 0mg
- Carbohydrates: 10g
- Fiber: 2g
- Sugar: 2g
- Sodium: 200mg

Ingredients:

- 2 tablespoons olive oil
- 1 large onion, chopped

- 3 cloves garlic, minced
- 3 carrots, chopped
- 2 celery stalks, chopped
- 2 cups mixed vegetables (e.g., zucchini, bell peppers, mushrooms)
- 6 cups water
- 2 teaspoons dried thyme
- 1 teaspoon dried bay leaves
- Salt and pepper, to taste
- Fresh herbs, for garnish (optional)

Directions:

1. In a large pot, heat the olive oil over medium heat.
2. Add the chopped onion, garlic, carrots, and celery, and sauté until the vegetables are tender (5-7 minutes).
3. Add the mixed vegetables and cook for an additional 2-3 minutes.
4. Pour in the water and add thyme and bay leaves.
5. Bring the mixture to a boil, then reduce heat to low and simmer for 20-25 minutes.
6. Strain the broth through a fine-mesh sieve or cheesecloth into a large bowl.
7. Discard the solids and season with salt and pepper to taste.
8. Serve hot, garnished with fresh herbs if desired.

Tips and Variations:

- For a clearer broth, use a coffee filter or paper towel to strain.
- Customize with your favorite vegetables or herbs.
- Store leftover broth in the refrigerator for up to 3 days or freeze for up to 2 months.

Chapter 4

Comforting Creamy Soups

Creamy Mushroom Soup

Servings: 4-6

Prep Time: 20 minutes

Cook Time: 25 minutes

Total Time: 45 minutes

Nutrition Information (per serving):

- Calories: 220
- Fat: 14g
- Saturated Fat: 8g
- Cholesterol: 40mg
- Sodium: 450mg
- Carbohydrates: 16g
- Fiber: 2g
- Sugar: 4g
- Protein: 10g

Ingredients:

- 2 tablespoons butter
- 1 medium onion, chopped
- 3 cups mixed mushrooms (button, cremini, shiitake), sliced
- 2 cloves garlic, minced
- 1 teaspoon dried thyme
- 1/2 teaspoon paprika
- 1/2 teaspoon salt
- 1/4 teaspoon black pepper
- 1 cup all-purpose flour
- 2 cups chicken broth
- 1 cup heavy cream
- Fresh parsley, chopped (optional)

Directions:

1. Melt butter in a large pot over medium heat.

2. Add onion and cook until softened, about 5 minutes.

3. Add mushrooms and cook until they release moisture and start browning, about 5-7 minutes.

4. Add garlic, thyme, paprika, salt, and pepper. Cook for 1 minute.

5. Sprinkle flour over mixture and cook for 1-2 minutes.

6. Gradually add chicken broth, whisking continuously. Bring to a boil, then reduce heat.

7. Simmer for 10-12 minutes or until soup thickens.

8. Stir in heavy cream.

9. Serve hot, garnished with chopped parsley if desired.

Tips and Variations:

- For an extra rich flavor, add 1/4 cup dry white wine before adding chicken broth.
- Substitute low-fat cream or half-and-half for a lighter version.
- Add diced chicken or bacon for added protein.
- Experiment with different mushroom varieties for unique flavors.

Sweet Potato and Coconut Soup

Servings: 4-6

Prep Time: 20 minutes

Cook Time: 30 minutes

Total Time: 50 minutes

Nutrition Information (per serving):

- Calories: 250
- Fat: 14g
- Saturated Fat: 12g

- Cholesterol: 0mg
- Sodium: 250mg
- Carbohydrates: 30g
- Fiber: 4g
- Sugar: 8g
- Protein: 2g

Ingredients:

- 2 large sweet potatoes, peeled and diced
- 2 tablespoons coconut oil
- 1 onion, chopped
- 3 cloves garlic, minced
- 1 teaspoon grated ginger
- 1 can (14 oz) coconut milk
- 2 cups vegetable broth
- 1 teaspoon ground cumin
- 1/2 teaspoon turmeric
- Salt and pepper, to taste
- Fresh cilantro, chopped (optional)

Directions:

1. In a large pot, heat coconut oil over medium heat.
2. Add onion, garlic, and ginger; cook until onion is translucent (5 minutes).
3. Add sweet potatoes, cumin, turmeric, salt, and pepper; cook for 5 minutes.
4. Pour in vegetable broth and bring to a boil.
5. Reduce heat, cover, and simmer until sweet potatoes are tender (15-20 minutes).
6. Use an immersion blender or transfer soup to a blender and puree until smooth.
7. Stir in coconut milk and adjust seasoning.
8. Serve hot, garnished with chopped cilantro if desired.

Tips and Variations:

- For a creamier soup, add more coconut milk or substitute with heavy cream.
- Add protein like cooked chicken or shrimp for added flavor.
- Spice up with red pepper flakes or sriracha for an extra kick.
- Serve with crusty bread or crackers for a filling meal.

Creamy Asparagus Soup

Servings: 4-6

Prep Time: 15 minutes

Cook Time: 20-25 minutes

Total Time: 35-40 minutes

Nutrition Information (per serving):

- Calories: 220
- Fat: 14g
- Saturated Fat: 8g
- Cholesterol: 30mg
- Sodium: 400mg
- Carbohydrates: 20g
- Fiber: 4g
- Protein: 10g

Ingredients:

- 2 pounds fresh asparagus, trimmed
- 2 tablespoons butter
- 1 medium onion, chopped
- 3 cloves garlic, minced
- 1/2 cup all-purpose flour
- 1 cup chicken or vegetable broth
- 1/2 cup heavy cream or half-and-half
- 1/2 cup grated Parmesan cheese (optional)
- Salt and pepper to taste
- Fresh parsley or chives for garnish (optional)

Directions:

1. In a large pot, melt butter over medium heat. Add chopped onion and cook until softened, about 5 minutes.

2. Add minced garlic and cook for 1 minute, until fragrant.

3. Add trimmed asparagus and cook for 5-7 minutes, or until tender.

4. Sprinkle flour over asparagus mixture and stir to combine. Cook for 1 minute.

5. Gradually pour in broth, whisking continuously to prevent lumps. Bring mixture to a simmer.

6. Reduce heat to low and let simmer for 10-12 minutes or until soup has thickened.

7. Use an immersion blender or transfer soup to a blender and puree until smooth.

8. Stir in heavy cream or half-and-half and Parmesan cheese (if using). Season with salt and pepper.

9. Serve hot, garnished with parsley or chives if desired.

Tips and Variations:

- For a lighter version, use less cream or substitute with Greek yogurt.
- Add cooked bacon, chicken, or shrimp for added protein.
- Experiment with different herbs and spices, such as nutmeg or paprika.
- Serve chilled or at room temperature for a refreshing summer soup.

Butternut Squash Soup

Servings: 4-6

Prep Time: 20 minutes

Cook Time: 40 minutes

Total Time: 1 hour

Nutrition Information (per serving):

- Calories: 180
- Fat: 9g
- Saturated Fat: 1.5g
- Cholesterol: 0mg
- Sodium: 400mg
- Carbohydrates: 25g
- Fiber: 4g
- Sugar: 8g
- Protein: 2g
- Vitamin A: 200% of the Daily Value (DV)

- Vitamin C: 40% of the DV

Ingredients:

- 1 large butternut squash (2-3 lbs)
- 2 tablespoons olive oil
- 1 onion, chopped
- 3 cloves garlic, minced
- 1 teaspoon ground cumin
- 1 teaspoon smoked paprika (optional)
- 1/2 teaspoon salt
- 1/4 teaspoon black pepper
- 4 cups vegetable broth
- 1/2 cup heavy cream or coconut cream (optional)
- Fresh herbs, such as parsley or sage, for garnish

Directions:

1. Preheat the oven to 400°F (200°C).
2. Peel, de-seed, and chop the butternut squash into 1-inch cubes.
3. Place the squash on a baking sheet, toss with 1 tablespoon olive oil, and roast for 30-40 minutes, or until tender.
4. In a large pot, heat the remaining 1 tablespoon olive oil over medium heat.
5. Add the chopped onion and cook until softened, about 5 minutes.
6. Add the minced garlic and cook for an additional 1-2 minutes.
7. Stir in the cumin, smoked paprika (if using), salt, and pepper.
8. Remove the roasted squash from the oven and add it to the pot.
9. Pour in the vegetable broth and bring the mixture to a boil.
10. Reduce heat and simmer for 15-20 minutes, or until the soup is heated through.
11. Use an immersion blender or transfer the soup to a blender and puree until smooth.
12. If desired, stir in the heavy cream or coconut cream for added creaminess.
13. Serve hot, garnished with fresh herbs.

Tips and Variations:

- For a creamier soup, add more heavy cream or coconut cream.
- Add a pinch of nutmeg or cinnamon for extra warmth.
- Use roasted garlic instead of raw garlic for deeper flavor.
- Serve with crusty bread or a swirl of creme fraiche.

Corn and Red Pepper Chowder

Servings: 6-8
Prep Time: 20 minutes
Cook Time: 30 minutes
Total Time: 50 minutes

Nutrition Information (per serving):

- Calories: 250
- Fat: 10g
- Saturated Fat: 2.5g
- Cholesterol: 20mg
- Sodium: 400mg
- Carbohydrates: 35g
- Fiber: 4g
- Protein: 15g

Ingredients:

- 2 tablespoons butter
- 1 medium onion, chopped
- 2 medium red bell peppers, chopped
- 2 cloves garlic, minced
- 1 cup corn kernels (fresh or frozen, thawed)
- 1 cup diced potatoes
- 1 cup chicken or vegetable broth
- 1/2 cup heavy cream or half-and-half (optional)
- 1 teaspoon paprika
- Salt and pepper, to taste
- Fresh cilantro or scallions, for garnish (optional)

Directions:

1. In a large pot or Dutch oven, melt butter over medium heat.
2. Add onion and cook until softened, about 5 minutes.
3. Add red peppers and cook for an additional 5 minutes.
4. Add garlic and cook for 1 minute.
5. Stir in corn, potatoes, broth, paprika, salt, and pepper.
6. Bring mixture to a boil, then reduce heat and simmer for 15-20 minutes, or until potatoes are tender.
7. Use an immersion blender or transfer soup to a blender and puree until slightly smooth.
8. If using heavy cream or half-and-half, stir in before serving.
9. Taste and adjust seasoning.

10. Serve hot, garnished with cilantro or scallions if desired.

Variations:

- Add diced cooked chicken or bacon for added protein.
- Substitute diced carrots or celery for added flavor.
- Use low-fat or non-dairy creamer for a healthier option.
- Serve with crusty bread or crackers for a satisfying meal.

Tips:

- Fresh corn kernels can be substituted with canned or frozen corn.
- Red peppers can be roasted in the oven before chopping for added depth of flavor.
- Chowder can be made ahead and refrigerated or frozen for later use.

Healthy Clam Chowder

Servings: 4-6

Prep Time: 20 minutes

Cook Time: 30 minutes

Total Time: 50 minutes

Nutrition Information (per serving):

- Calories: 220
- Protein: 17g
- Fat: 10g
- Saturated Fat: 1.5g
- Cholesterol: 30mg
- Sodium: 450mg
- Carbohydrates: 20g
- Fiber: 2g
- Sugar: 2g

Ingredients:

- 2 tablespoons olive oil
- 1 medium onion, diced

- 2 cloves garlic, minced
- 1 medium celery stalk, diced
- 1 medium potato, peeled and diced
- 1 can (14.5 oz) diced tomatoes
- 1 cup low-sodium chicken broth
- 1/2 cup low-fat milk
- 1 teaspoon dried thyme
- 1/2 teaspoon paprika
- 1/4 teaspoon cayenne pepper (optional)
- 1 pound fresh or canned clams, drained and rinsed
- Salt and pepper to taste
- Fresh parsley, chopped (for garnish)

Directions:

1. Heat olive oil in a large pot over medium heat.

2. Add onion, garlic, and celery; cook until tender (5-7 minutes).

3. Add potato, diced tomatoes, chicken broth, milk, thyme, paprika, and cayenne pepper (if using). Bring to a boil, then reduce heat and simmer (15-20 minutes or until potatoes are tender).

4. Stir in clams and cook until heated through.

5. Season with salt and pepper.

6. Serve hot, garnished with parsley.

Tips and Variations:

- For a creamier chowder, add 1-2 tablespoons low-fat cream or Greek yogurt.
- Substitute diced bell peppers or carrots for added flavor and nutrients.
- Use fresh clams for the best flavor, or canned for convenience.
- Make it a Manhattan-style clam chowder by adding 1-2 tablespoons tomato paste.

Chapter 5

Immune Boosting Soups

Garlic and Chicken Soup

Servings: 4-6

Prep Time: 15 minutes

Cook Time: 30 minutes

Total Time: 45 minutes

Nutrition Information (per serving):

- Calories: 220
- Protein: 26g
- Fat: 8g
- Saturated Fat: 2.5g
- Cholesterol: 60mg
- Carbohydrates: 20g
- Fiber: 2g
- Sugar: 2g
- Sodium: 450mg

Ingredients:

- 1 pound boneless, skinless chicken breast or thighs
- 4 cloves garlic, minced
- 2 medium onions, chopped
- 3 carrots, peeled and sliced
- 2 celery stalks, sliced
- 4 cups chicken broth
- 2 cups water
- 1 teaspoon dried thyme
- 1/2 teaspoon dried basil
- Salt and pepper, to taste
- 2 tablespoons olive oil (optional)

Directions:

1. In a large pot or Dutch oven, heat the olive oil over medium heat.
2. Add the chopped onions, carrots, and celery and cook until the vegetables are tender, about 5-7 minutes.
3. Add the minced garlic and cook for an additional 1-2 minutes, until fragrant.
4. Add the chicken to the pot and cook until browned on all sides, about 5-6 minutes.
5. Pour in the chicken broth, water, thyme, and basil. Bring the mixture to a boil, then reduce the heat to low and simmer.
6. Let the soup simmer for 15-20 minutes or until the chicken is cooked through.
7. Season the soup with salt and pepper to taste.
8. Serve hot, garnished with chopped fresh herbs if desired.

Tips and Variations:

- For a creamier soup, add 1/4 cup heavy cream or half-and-half.
- Add noodles, rice, or potatoes for added texture.
- Use roasted garlic for a deeper flavor.
- Substitute chicken with turkey or vegetables for a vegetarian option.

Storage and Reheating:

- Store leftovers in an airtight container in the refrigerator for up to 3 days.
- Reheat the soup over low heat, stirring occasionally.

Spiced Turmeric Lentil Soup

Servings: 4-6

Prep Time: 20 minutes

Cook Time: 30-40 minutes

Total Time: 50-60 minutes

Nutrition Information (per serving):

- Calories: 250
- Protein: 18g
- Fat: 9g
- Saturated Fat: 1g
- Carbohydrates: 30g
- Fiber: 10g
- Sugar: 2g

- Sodium: 400mg

Ingredients:

- 1 cup brown or green lentils, rinsed and drained
- 2 tablespoons olive oil
- 1 onion, chopped
- 2 cloves garlic, minced
- 1 carrot, chopped
- 1 celery stalk, chopped
- 1 teaspoon ground cumin
- 1 teaspoon ground coriander
- 1/2 teaspoon turmeric powder
- 1/2 teaspoon cayenne pepper (optional)
- 1 can (14.5 oz) diced tomatoes
- 4 cups vegetable broth
- 1 can (14 oz) coconut milk (optional)
- Salt and pepper, to taste
- Fresh cilantro, chopped (for garnish)

Directions:

1. In a large pot, heat olive oil over medium heat.
2. Add onion, garlic, carrot, and celery; cook until vegetables are tender, about 5-7 minutes.
3. Stir in cumin, coriander, turmeric, and cayenne pepper (if using); cook for 1 minute.
4. Add lentils, diced tomatoes, and vegetable broth; bring to a boil.
5. Reduce heat, cover, and simmer for 20-25 minutes or until lentils are tender.
6. Use an immersion blender to puree soup partially, or leave as is.
7. If using coconut milk, stir it in during the last 5 minutes of cooking.
8. Season with salt and pepper to taste.
9. Serve hot, garnished with chopped cilantro.

Tips and Variations:

- For a creamier soup, add more coconut milk or substitute with Greek yogurt.
- Add spinach or kale for extra nutrients.
- Use red or yellow lentils for a slightly different texture.
- Serve with crusty bread or over rice.

Ginger and Carrot Soup

Servings: 4-6 people

Prep Time: 20 minutes

Cook Time: 30 minutes

Total Time: 50 minutes

Nutrition Information (per serving):

- Calories: 140
- Protein: 2g
- Fat: 7g
- Saturated Fat: 1g
- Cholesterol: 0mg
- Carbohydrates: 22g
- Fiber: 4g
- Sugar: 6g
- Sodium: 400mg

Ingredients:

- 2 medium onions, chopped
- 3 cloves garlic, minced
- 2 inches fresh ginger, peeled and grated
- 6 medium carrots, peeled and chopped
- 4 cups vegetable broth
- 1 cup coconut milk or heavy cream (optional)
- 1 tsp ground cumin
- 1 tsp smoked paprika (optional)
- Salt and pepper, to taste
- Fresh cilantro or scallions, for garnish

Directions:

1. In a large pot, heat 2 tbsp olive oil over medium heat.
2. Add chopped onions and cook until softened, about 5 minutes.
3. Add minced garlic and grated ginger; cook for 1 minute.
4. Add chopped carrots, vegetable broth, cumin, smoked paprika (if using), salt, and pepper.
5. Bring to a boil, then reduce heat and simmer until carrots are tender, about 20-25 minutes.
6. Use an immersion blender or transfer soup to a blender and puree until smooth.

7. If desired, stir in coconut milk or heavy cream for added creaminess.
8. Taste and adjust seasoning.
9. Serve hot, garnished with fresh cilantro or scallions.

Tips and Variations:

- For extra flavor, roast carrots in the oven at 425°F (220°C) for 20-25 minutes before adding to soup.
- Substitute coconut milk with Greek yogurt or sour cream for a tangier taste.
- Add protein like cooked chicken or tofu for added nutrition.
- Experiment with spices, such as cayenne pepper or ground turmeric, for unique flavor profiles.

Immune Boosting Vegetable Soup

Servings: 4-6

Prep Time: 20 minutes

Cook Time: 30 minutes

Total Time: 50 minutes

Nutrition Information (per serving):

- Calories: 220
- Protein: 15g
- Fat: 8g
- Saturated Fat: 1g
- Cholesterol: 0mg
- Carbohydrates: 35g
- Fiber: 5g
- Sugar: 10g
- Sodium: 400mg

Ingredients:

- 2 tablespoons olive oil
- 1 onion, diced
- 3 cloves garlic, minced
- 2 medium carrots, peeled and sliced
- 2 stalks celery, sliced
- 2 cups mixed mushrooms (shiitake, cremini, bell)
- 2 cups chopped kale

- 2 cups diced tomatoes
- 4 cups vegetable broth (low-sodium)
- 1 teaspoon dried thyme
- 1 teaspoon dried oregano
- 1/2 teaspoon ground cumin
- Salt and pepper, to taste
- 1/4 teaspoon red pepper flakes (optional)
- 2 tablespoons freshly squeezed lemon juice

Directions:

1. In a large pot, heat the olive oil over medium heat.
2. Add onion, garlic, carrots, and celery; cook until tender (8-10 minutes).
3. Add mushrooms; cook until they release moisture and start browning (5 minutes).
4. Stir in kale, diced tomatoes, vegetable broth, thyme, oregano, cumin, salt, pepper, and red pepper flakes (if using).
5. Bring to a boil, then reduce heat and simmer for 15-20 minutes or until vegetables are tender.
6. Stir in lemon juice.
7. Serve hot, garnished with fresh herbs (optional).

Immune-Boosting Benefits:

- Vitamin C-rich kale and tomatoes support immune function.
- Antioxidant-rich carrots and mushrooms combat free radicals.
- Garlic's active compound, allicin, has antimicrobial properties.
- Lemon juice provides an extra boost of vitamin C.

Tips and Variations:

- Customize with your favorite vegetables.
- Add protein sources like beans, lentils, or chicken for added nutrition.
- Store leftovers in the refrigerator for up to 3 days or freeze for up to 2 months.
- Experiment with spices and herbs to create unique flavor profiles.

Lemon and Herb Broth

Servings: 4-6

Prep Time: 15 minutes

Cook Time: 20-25 minutes

Total Time: 35-40 minutes

Nutrition Information (per serving):

- Calories: 60
- Protein: 2g
- Fat: 0g
- Saturated Fat: 0g
- Cholesterol: 0mg
- Carbohydrates: 14g
- Fiber: 2g
- Sugar: 2g
- Sodium: 400mg

Ingredients:

- 4 cups vegetable or chicken broth (low-sodium)
- 2 lemons, sliced
- 1/4 cup fresh parsley, chopped
- 1/4 cup fresh mint, chopped
- 2 tbsp olive oil
- 2 cloves garlic, minced
- 1 tsp dried thyme
- 1 tsp dried rosemary
- Salt and pepper to taste
- 1/2 tsp lemon zest (optional)

Directions:

1. In a large pot, heat the olive oil over medium heat.
2. Add garlic and sauté for 1-2 minutes until fragrant.
3. Add broth, lemon slices, parsley, mint, thyme, and rosemary.
4. Bring mixture to a boil, then reduce heat to low and simmer for 15-20 minutes.
5. Season with salt and pepper to taste.
6. Strain broth and discard solids.
7. Serve hot, garnished with lemon zest if desired.

Tips and Variations:

- For an extra burst of citrus flavor, squeeze lemon juice into the broth before serving.
- Add protein like chicken or tofu for a heartier meal.
- Experiment with different herbs like basil or oregano for unique flavor profiles.
- Store leftover broth in the refrigerator for up to 3 days or freeze for up to 2 months.

Green Detox Soup

Servings: 4-6

Prep Time: 20 minutes

Cook Time: 30 minutes

Total Time: 50 minutes

Nutrition Information (per serving):

Calories: 170
Protein: 5g
Fat: 7g
Saturated Fat: 1g
Cholesterol: 0mg
Carbohydrates: 25g
Fiber: 5g
Sugar: 5g
Sodium: 200mg

Ingredients:

- 2 tablespoons olive oil
- 1 onion, chopped
- 3 cloves garlic, minced
- 2 cups chopped kale
- 2 cups chopped spinach
- 1 cup chopped green beans
- 1 cup diced zucchini
- 4 cups vegetable broth
- 1 cup diced cucumber
- 1/2 cup freshly squeezed lemon juice
- 1 teaspoon grated ginger
- Salt and pepper to taste
- Optional: 1/4 teaspoon cayenne pepper

Directions:

1. Heat the olive oil in a large pot over medium heat.

2. Add the chopped onion and sauté until softened, about 5 minutes.

3. Add the minced garlic and cook for an additional minute.

1. Add the chopped kale, spinach, green beans, zucchini, and vegetable broth.

2. Bring the mixture to a boil, then reduce heat and simmer for 20 minutes.

3. Stir in the diced cucumber, lemon juice, grated ginger, salt, pepper, and cayenne pepper (if using).

4. Continue to simmer for an additional 5-10 minutes.

5. Use an immersion blender to puree the soup until smooth, or allow it to cool and puree in a blender.

6. Serve hot and enjoy!

Tips and Variations:

- For an extra creamy soup, add 1/4 cup Greek yogurt or coconut cream.
- Substitute other leafy greens like collard greens or Swiss chard for kale and spinach.
- Add 1/2 cup cooked quinoa or brown rice for added protein and fiber.
- Experiment with different spices, such as cumin or paprika, for unique flavor profiles.

This Green Detox Soup is packed with nutrient-dense ingredients to support overall health and well-being. The combination of leafy greens, vegetables, and citrus provides a refreshing and rejuvenating culinary experience.

Chapter 6

International Flavors

Thai Coconut Chicken Soup

Serving Size: 4-6

Cooking Time: 20-25 minutes

Prep Time: 10-15 minutes

Nutrition Information (per serving):

- Calories: 320
- Protein: 24g
- Fat: 22g
- Saturated Fat: 14g
- Cholesterol: 60mg
- Sodium: 450mg
- Carbohydrates: 12g
- Fiber: 2g
- Sugar: 6g

Ingredients:

- 2 tablespoons vegetable oil
- 1 onion, thinly sliced
- 2 cloves garlic, minced
- 1 tablespoon grated fresh ginger
- 1 pound boneless, skinless chicken breast or thighs, cut into bite-sized pieces
- 2 cups chicken broth
- 1 can (14 oz) coconut milk
- 1 tablespoon Thai red curry paste
- 1 teaspoon fish sauce (optional)
- 1/2 teaspoon ground cumin
- 1/2 teaspoon salt
- 1/4 teaspoon black pepper
- 2 cups mixed mushrooms (button, shiitake, bell), sliced
- 1/4 cup chopped fresh cilantro (for garnish)
- Lime wedges (for serving)

Directions:

1. Heat oil in a large pot over medium-high heat. Add onion and cook until softened, 3-4 minutes.

2. Add garlic and ginger; cook 1 minute.

3. Add chicken and cook until browned, 5-6 minutes.

4. Pour in chicken broth, coconut milk, curry paste, fish sauce (if using), cumin, salt, and pepper. Stir to combine.

5. Bring mixture to a simmer. Reduce heat to medium-low and cook 10-12 minutes or until chicken is cooked through.

6. Add mushrooms and cook 3-4 minutes or until tender.

7. Taste and adjust seasoning.

1. Ladle soup into bowls and garnish with cilantro. Serve with lime wedges.

Optional Variations:

- Add noodles or rice for a heartier meal.
- Substitute chicken with shrimp or tofu for a vegetarian/vegan option.
- Adjust spice level to taste by adding more curry paste or using sriracha.

Mexican Tortilla Soup

Servings: 6-8
Cooking Time: 30-40 minutes
Prep Time: 15-20 minutes
Nutrition Information (per serving):

- Calories: 250
- Fat: 10g
- Saturated Fat: 2.5g
- Cholesterol: 20mg
- Sodium: 400mg
- Carbohydrates: 30g
- Fiber: 5g
- Protein: 20g

Ingredients:

- 1 lb boneless, skinless chicken breast or thighs, cut into bite-sized pieces
- 2 tablespoons olive oil
- 1 large onion, diced
- 3 cloves garlic, minced
- 1 red bell pepper, diced
- 2 teaspoons ground cumin
- 1 teaspoon smoked paprika
- 1/2 teaspoon cayenne pepper (optional)
- 1 can (14.5 oz) diced tomatoes, drained
- 4 cups chicken broth
- 6-8 corn tortillas, cut into thin strips
- 1/2 cup shredded cheese (Monterey Jack or Cheddar)
- 1/4 cup chopped fresh cilantro
- Salt and pepper, to taste
- Lime wedges, for serving

Directions:

1. In a large pot, heat olive oil over medium-high heat.
2. Add chicken and cook until browned, about 5-7 minutes. Remove from pot and set aside.
3. Add onion, garlic, and red bell pepper to pot. Cook until vegetables are tender, about 5 minutes.
4. Stir in cumin, smoked paprika, and cayenne pepper (if using). Cook for 1 minute.
5. Add diced tomatoes, chicken broth, and browned chicken back to pot. Bring to a boil, then reduce heat to low and simmer for 15-20 minutes.
6. Meanwhile, preheat oven to 400°F (200°C). Place tortilla strips on a baking sheet and bake for 10-12 minutes, or until crispy.
7. To serve, ladle soup into bowls and top with tortilla strips, shredded cheese, and chopped cilantro.
8. Serve with lime wedges on the side.

Optional Toppings:

- Diced avocado
- Sour cream
- Sliced radishes
- Chopped scallions
- Crushed tortilla chips

Tips and Variations:

- Use leftover chicken or turkey for added convenience.
- Substitute diced bell peppers with diced jalapeños for extra heat.

- Add a can of black beans or diced potatoes for added fiber and protein.
- For a vegetarian version, replace chicken with roasted vegetables or tofu.

Indian Spiced Lentil Soup

Servings: 4-6

Cooking Time: 30-40 minutes

Prep Time: 15-20 minutes

Nutrition Information (per serving):

- Calories: 250
- Protein: 18g
- Fat: 9g
- Saturated Fat: 1g
- Carbohydrates: 35g
- Fiber: 10g
- Sugar: 5g
- Sodium: 400mg
- Cholesterol: 0mg

Ingredients:

- 1 cup split red or yellow lentils (masoor dal), rinsed and drained
- 2 medium onions, chopped
- 3 cloves garlic, minced
- 1 medium ginger, grated
- 1 tablespoon ghee or vegetable oil
- 1 teaspoon ground cumin
- 1 teaspoon ground coriander
- 1/2 teaspoon turmeric
- 1/2 teaspoon cayenne pepper (optional)
- 1/2 teaspoon salt
- 1/4 teaspoon black pepper
- 4 cups vegetable broth
- 2 cups water
- 2 medium tomatoes, diced
- Fresh cilantro, chopped (for garnish)
- Lemon wedges (for serving)

Directions:

1. In a large pot, heat the ghee or oil over medium heat.
2. Add the onions and cook until softened, 5 minutes.
3. Add the garlic and ginger; cook for 1 minute.
4. Stir in cumin, coriander, turmeric, cayenne pepper (if using), salt, and black pepper. Cook for 1 minute.
5. Add the lentils, vegetable broth, water, and diced tomatoes.
6. Bring to a boil, then reduce heat to low and simmer, covered, for 20-25 minutes or until lentils are tender.
7. Use an immersion blender to puree the soup partially, or leave it chunky.
8. Taste and adjust seasoning.
9. Serve hot, garnished with cilantro and accompanied by lemon wedges.

Variations:

- Add spinach or kale for extra nutrition.
- Use coconut milk for creaminess.
- Substitute split green lentils or chickpeas for variation.
- Serve with naan or rice for a filling meal.

Tips:

- Red lentils break down quickly, while yellow lentils hold shape.
- Adjust spice level to your preference.
- Make ahead and refrigerate or freeze for up to 3 days.

Italian Minestrone Soup

Servings: 6-8

Prep Time: 20 minutes

Cook Time: 40 minutes

Total Time: 1 hour

Nutrition Information (per serving):

- Calories: 220
- Fat: 9g
- Saturated Fat: 1.5g

- Cholesterol: 0mg
- Sodium: 450mg
- Carbohydrates: 30g
- Fiber: 6g
- Protein: 12g

Ingredients:

- 1 tablespoon olive oil
- 1 onion, chopped
- 3 cloves garlic, minced
- 2 medium carrots, chopped
- 2 celery stalks, chopped
- 1 (14.5 oz) can diced tomatoes
- 4 cups vegetable broth
- 1 can kidney beans, drained and rinsed
- 1 can cannellini beans, drained and rinsed
- 1 cup small pasta shapes (e.g., elbow macaroni)
- 1 teaspoon dried basil
- 1 teaspoon dried oregano
- Salt and pepper, to taste
- Grated Parmesan cheese, for serving (optional)

Directions:

1. Heat olive oil in a large pot over medium heat.
2. Add onion, garlic, carrots, and celery; cook until vegetables are tender (8-10 minutes).
3. Add diced tomatoes, vegetable broth, kidney beans, cannellini beans, pasta, basil, oregano, salt, and pepper.
4. Bring to a boil, then reduce heat and simmer for 20-25 minutes or until pasta is al dente.
5. Taste and adjust seasoning.
6. Serve hot, topped with grated Parmesan cheese if desired.

Tips and Variations:

- Customize with your favorite vegetables or beans.
- Add ground beef or sausage for added protein.
- Serve with crusty bread or a side salad.
- Refrigerate or freeze for later use.

French Onion Soup

Servings: 4-6
Prep Time: 20 minutes
Cook Time: 30 minutes
Total Time: 50 minutes

Nutrition Information (per serving):

- Calories: 220
- Fat: 8g
- Saturated Fat: 1.5g
- Cholesterol: 20mg
- Sodium: 400mg
- Carbohydrates: 25g
- Fiber: 2g
- Protein: 15g

Ingredients:

- 2 tablespoons olive oil
- 1 medium onion, diced
- 2 cloves garlic, minced
- 1 medium potato, peeled and diced
- 1 cup clam juice (low-sodium)
- 1/2 cup non-fat milk
- 1/2 cup diced fresh clams (or canned)
- 1 teaspoon dried thyme
- 1/2 teaspoon paprika
- Salt and pepper to taste
- 2 tablespoons chopped fresh parsley (optional)

Directions:

1. Heat oil in a large pot over medium heat.
2. Add onion and cook until softened (5 minutes).
3. Add garlic and cook for 1 minute.
4. Add potato, clam juice, milk, thyme, paprika, salt, and pepper. Bring to a simmer.
5. Reduce heat and cook until potatoes are tender (15 minutes).
6. Stir in clams and cook until heated through.
7. Taste and adjust seasoning.
8. Serve hot, garnished with parsley if desired.

Health Tips:

- Use low-sodium clam juice to reduce sodium content.
- Choose non-fat milk to reduce saturated fat.
- Fresh clams provide lean protein and omega-3 fatty acids.
- Potato adds fiber and complex carbohydrates.

Variations:

- Add diced bell peppers or celery for extra flavor and nutrients.
- Use canned clams for convenience.
- Substitute Greek yogurt for non-fat milk for added creaminess.

Japanese Miso Soup

Servings: 4-6 people

Prep Time: 10 minutes

Cook Time: 15-20 minutes

Total Time: 25-30 minutes

Nutrition Information (per serving):

- Calories: 90
- Protein: 4g
- Fat: 4g
- Saturated Fat: 0.5g
- Cholesterol: 0mg
- Carbohydrates: 12g
- Fiber: 2g
- Sugar: 4g
- Sodium: 450mg

Ingredients:

- 2 cups dashi broth (or vegetable broth)
- 2 tablespoons miso paste
- 1 tablespoon soy sauce
- 1 teaspoon grated ginger
- 2 cloves garlic, minced

- 1/4 cup sliced shiitake mushrooms
- 1/4 cup sliced green onions
- 1/4 cup cubed tofu (optional)
- Sesame seeds and chopped scallions for garnish (optional)

Directions:

1. In a large pot, combine dashi broth, soy sauce, ginger, and garlic. Bring to a simmer over medium heat.

2. Reduce heat to low and add miso paste. Whisk until dissolved.

3. Add mushrooms and cook until tender, about 5 minutes.

4. Add green onions and tofu (if using). Cook for an additional 2-3 minutes.

5. Taste and adjust seasoning.

6. Serve hot, garnished with sesame seeds and chopped scallions (if desired).

Tips and Variations:

- For a vegetarian version, use vegetable broth instead of dashi.
- Add noodles or rice for a heartier meal.
- Experiment with different types of miso paste for varying flavors.
- Customize with your favorite protein sources, such as shrimp or chicken.

Dashi Broth Recipe (optional):

- 4 cups water
- 2 cups kombu seaweed
- 1 cup katsuobushi (dried bonito flakes)

Combine water and kombu in a pot. Bring to a boil, then reduce heat and simmer for 10 minutes. Remove kombu and add katsuobushi. Simmer for an additional 5 minutes. Strain and use in miso soup recipe.

Chapter 7

Quick and Easy Soups

15 Minute Tomato Basil Soup

Servings: 4-6

Prep Time: 5 minutes

Cook Time: 10 minutes

Total Time: 15 minutes

Nutrition Information (per serving):

- Calories: 120
- Fat: 7g
- Saturated Fat: 1g
- Cholesterol: 0mg
- Sodium: 400mg
- Carbohydrates: 18g
- Fiber: 4g
- Sugar: 10g
- Protein: 3g

Ingredients:

- 2 cups chopped fresh tomatoes (or 1 can of diced tomatoes)
- 1 cup chicken or vegetable broth
- 1/4 cup fresh basil leaves, chopped
- 2 cloves garlic, minced
- 1 tablespoon olive oil
- 1 teaspoon dried oregano
- Salt and pepper, to taste
- 1/2 cup heavy cream or half-and-half (optional)
- Grated Parmesan cheese, for serving (optional)

Directions:

1. In a large pot, heat the olive oil over medium heat.
2. Add the minced garlic and cook for 1 minute, until fragrant.

3. Add the chopped tomatoes, broth, basil, and oregano. Stir to combine.
4. Bring the mixture to a boil, then reduce heat to low and simmer for 5 minutes.
5. Use an immersion blender to puree the soup until smooth. Alternatively, transfer the soup to a blender and blend until smooth, then return to pot.
6. Season with salt and pepper to taste.
7. If desired, stir in heavy cream or half-and-half to add creaminess.
8. Serve hot, topped with grated Parmesan cheese if desired.

Tips:

- Use fresh, high-quality ingredients for the best flavor.
- For an extra boost of flavor, add 1-2 tablespoons of tomato paste.
- Serve with crusty bread or crackers for dipping.
- Refrigerate or freeze leftover soup for up to 3 days.

Instant Pot Vegetable Soup

Servings: 4-6

Prep Time: 15 minutes

Cook Time: 10 minutes

Total Time: 25 minutes

Nutrition Information (per serving):

- Calories: 120
- Fat: 2g
- Saturated Fat: 0.5g
- Cholesterol: 0mg
- Sodium: 400mg
- Carbohydrates: 25g
- Fiber: 5g
- Sugar: 6g
- Protein: 3g

Ingredients:

- 2 tablespoons olive oil
- 1 onion, chopped
- 3 cloves garlic, minced

- 3 carrots, peeled and chopped
- 2 celery stalks, chopped
- 2 cups mixed vegetables (e.g., zucchini, bell peppers, green beans)
- 4 cups vegetable broth
- 1 can (14.5 oz) diced tomatoes
- 1 teaspoon dried thyme
- 1 teaspoon dried basil
- Salt and pepper, to taste
- Fresh parsley, chopped (optional)

Directions:

1. Press the "Saute" button on the Instant Pot and heat the olive oil.
2. Add the chopped onion and cook until softened, about 3-4 minutes.
3. Add the minced garlic and cook for an additional minute.
4. Add the chopped carrots and celery and cook for 2-3 minutes.
5. Add the mixed vegetables, vegetable broth, diced tomatoes, thyme, and basil.
6. Season with salt and pepper to taste.
7. Close the lid and set the valve to "Sealing".
8. Press the "Manual" or "Pressure Cook" button and set the cooking time to 5 minutes at high pressure.
9. When the cooking time is up, allow the pressure to release naturally for 5 minutes, then quick-release any remaining pressure.
10. Serve hot, garnished with chopped fresh parsley if desired.

Tips and Variations:

- Customize the recipe with your favorite vegetables.
- Add protein sources like cooked chicken, beans, or tofu for added nutrition.
- For a creamier soup, add 1/4 cup heavy cream or coconut cream.
- Experiment with different herbs and spices to change the flavor profile.

Quick Chickpea and Spinach Stew

Servings: 4-6

Prep Time: 15 minutes

Cook Time: 20 minutes

Total Time: 35 minutes

Nutrition Information (per serving):

- Calories: 250
- Protein: 15g
- Fat: 10g
- Saturated Fat: 1g
- Cholesterol: 0mg
- Carbohydrates: 30g
- Fiber: 5g
- Sugar: 5g
- Sodium: 400mg

Ingredients:

- 1 tablespoon olive oil
- 1 onion, chopped
- 2 cloves garlic, minced
- 1 teaspoon ground cumin
- 1 teaspoon smoked paprika
- 1/2 teaspoon salt
- 1/4 teaspoon black pepper
- 1 can chickpeas (14.5 oz), drained and rinsed
- 2 cups vegetable broth
- 1 can diced tomatoes (14.5 oz)
- 2 cups fresh spinach leaves
- 2 tablespoons lemon juice
- Optional: feta cheese, crusty bread, or naan for serving

Directions:

1. Heat the olive oil in a large pot over medium heat.

2. Add the onion and cook, stirring occasionally, until softened (5 minutes).

3. Add the garlic, cumin, smoked paprika, salt, and pepper; cook for 1 minute.

4. Stir in the chickpeas, vegetable broth, and diced tomatoes.

5. Bring the mixture to a simmer.

6. Reduce heat to low and let cook for 15 minutes.

7. Stir in the spinach leaves until wilted.

8. Add lemon juice and adjust seasoning.

9. Serve hot, topped with feta cheese and crusty bread or naan, if desired.

Tips and Variations:

- For added protein, include cooked chicken, sausage, or tofu.
- Substitute kale or collard greens for spinach.
- Add diced bell peppers or carrots for extra flavor and nutrients.
- Serve over rice, quinoa, or with warm pita bread.

Fast Lentil and Carrot Soup

Servings: 4-6

Prep Time: 15 minutes

Cook Time: 25 minutes

Total Time: 40 minutes

Nutrition Information (per serving):

- Calories: 230
- Protein: 18g
- Fat: 9g
- Saturated Fat: 1g
- Cholesterol: 0mg
- Carbohydrates: 30g
- Fiber: 10g
- Sugar: 6g
- Sodium: 400mg

Ingredients:

- 1 cup dried green or brown lentils, rinsed and drained
- 2 medium carrots, chopped
- 2 cloves garlic, minced
- 1 medium onion, chopped
- 2 cups vegetable broth
- 1 cup water
- 1 can (14.5 oz) diced tomatoes

- 1 teaspoon ground cumin
- 1 teaspoon smoked paprika (optional)
- Salt and pepper, to taste
- 2 tablespoons olive oil
- Fresh cilantro or parsley, chopped (for garnish)

Directions:

1. In a large pot, heat the olive oil over medium heat.
2. Add the onion and cook until softened, about 5 minutes.
3. Add the garlic and cook for 1 minute.
4. Add the carrots and cook for 2-3 minutes.
5. Add the lentils, vegetable broth, water, diced tomatoes, cumin, smoked paprika (if using), salt, and pepper.
6. Bring to a boil, then reduce heat to low and simmer, covered, for 20 minutes or until the lentils are tender.
7. Use an immersion blender to puree the soup to desired consistency.
8. Taste and adjust seasoning.
9. Serve hot, garnished with chopped cilantro or parsley.

Tips:

- For a creamier soup, add 1/4 cup coconut cream or Greek yogurt.
- Add spinach or kale for extra nutrients.
- Serve with crusty bread or over rice.

Speedy Potato and Leek Soup

Servings: 4-6

Prep Time: 15 minutes

Cook Time: 20 minutes

Total Time: 35 minutes

Nutrition Information (per serving):

- Calories: 220
- Fat: 8g
- Saturated Fat: 1.5g
- Cholesterol: 10mg

- Sodium: 450mg
- Carbohydrates: 35g
- Fiber: 4g
- Protein: 5g

Ingredients:

- 2 large potatoes, peeled and diced
- 2 medium leeks, cleaned and chopped (white and light green parts)
- 2 tablespoons butter
- 1 onion, chopped
- 4 cups chicken or vegetable broth
- 1/2 cup heavy cream or half-and-half (optional)
- Salt and pepper to taste
- Fresh parsley or chives for garnish

Directions:

1. In a large pot, melt butter over medium heat.
2. Add chopped onion and cook until softened, about 3-4 minutes.
3. Add chopped leeks and cook for an additional 5 minutes, or until tender.
4. Add diced potatoes, broth, salt, and pepper. Bring to a boil, then reduce heat and simmer for 15-20 minutes, or until potatoes are tender.
5. Use an immersion blender or transfer soup to a blender and puree until smooth.
6. If desired, stir in heavy cream or half-and-half for added richness.
7. Taste and adjust seasoning.
8. Serve hot, garnished with fresh parsley or chives.

Tips:

- Use the white and light green parts of the leeks for the best flavor.
- For a creamier soup, add more heavy cream or half-and-half.
- Serve with crusty bread or crackers for a satisfying meal.

Variations:

- Add diced ham, bacon, or cooked chicken for added protein.
- Use garlic or celery for added depth of flavor.
- Experiment with different herbs, such as thyme or rosemary, for a unique twist.

Rapid Fire Gazpacho

Servings: 4-6

Prep Time: 15 minutes

Cook Time: 0 minutes (chilled)

Total Time: 15 minutes

Nutrition Information (per serving):

- Calories: 120
- Protein: 3g
- Fat: 7g
- Saturated Fat: 1g
- Cholesterol: 0mg
- Carbohydrates: 18g
- Fiber: 4g
- Sugar: 8g
- Sodium: 250mg
- Potassium: 450mg
- Vitamin A: 20% DV
- Vitamin C: 100% DV

Ingredients:

- 2 cups diced fresh tomatoes (or 1 can of diced tomatoes)
- 1 cup diced bell pepper
- 1 cup diced cucumber
- 1/2 cup diced red onion
- 1/4 cup extra-virgin olive oil
- 2 cloves garlic, minced
- 2 tablespoons sherry vinegar
- 1 teaspoon smoked paprika
- Salt and pepper, to taste
- 1/4 cup chopped fresh cilantro (optional)

Directions:

1. In a blender or food processor, combine tomatoes, bell pepper, cucumber, onion, garlic, olive oil, vinegar, smoked paprika, salt, and pepper.
2. Blend until smooth, stopping to scrape down sides as needed.

3. Taste and adjust seasoning.
4. Chill in the refrigerator for at least 10 minutes.
5. Serve cold, garnished with chopped cilantro if desired.

Tips and Variations:

- Use fresh, seasonal ingredients for the best flavor.
- Add a diced jalapeño for an extra kick.
- Serve with crusty bread or grilled cheese croutons.
- Experiment with different types of tomatoes, such as cherry or grape tomatoes.

Made in the USA
Monee, IL
19 May 2025

17742780R00044